ENCYCLOPEDIA of PRESIDENTS

William Jefferson Clinton

Forty-Second President of the United States

By Zachary Kent

Consultant: Charles Abele, Ph.D.
Social Studies Instructor
Chicago Public School System

 CHILDRENS PRESS®
CHICAGO

Hillary Rodham Clinton and Bill Clinton

Library of Congress Cataloging-in-Publication Data

Kent, Zachary.
    Bill Clinton / by Zachary Kent.
        p.   cm. — (Encyclopedia of presidents)
    Includes index.
    Summary: A biography of the Arkansas governor who became
the forty-second president of the United States.
    ISBN 0-516-01350-5
    1. Clinton, Bill, 1946-   —Juvenile literature.
2. Presidents—United States—Biography—Juvenile
literature. [1. Clinton, Bill, 1946-   . 2. Presidents.]
I. Title. II. Series.
E886.K46   1993
973.929$092—dc20   92-47044
[B]   CIP
[92]   AC

Picture Acknowledgments

Cover—Courtesy the White House

AP/Wide World Photos, Inc.—2, 4, 5, 9, 31, 35,
45, 46, 48, 51, 53, 54, 55, 57, 58, 60, 61, 63, 64
(both photos), 66, 68 (top), 69 (both photos), 70,
73, 76, 77, 82, 84 (top), 86, 89

Courtesy Donna Taylor Wingfield—14, 15
(bottom)

Courtesy Georgetown University—28, 30

Courtesy Hot Springs High School, photographed
by Tim Estes—19 (both photos), 20, 24-25 (all
photos), 26

Courtesy Mrs. June Downs—15, (top)

Courtesy Office of the President-Elect and Vice-
President-Elect—23

Courtesy Tim Estes—10, 13, 21

Courtesy University of Arkansas—40

Courtesy Yale Law School—33

© Tim Estes—12

UPI/Bettmann Newsphotos—6, 8, 36, 42, 43,
47, 68 (bottom), 77 (both photos), 78, 81, 83

The new president delivers his inaugural address on January 20, 1993.

Table of Contents

Chapter 1

Victory!

On the evening of November 3, 1992, in Little Rock, Arkansas, excited men and women hugged each other and danced in the streets. Thousands of people had arrived that day by bus, plane, and automobile. They wanted to be there to celebrate Arkansas governor Bill Clinton's election as president of the United States.

Inside their headquarters, Democratic campaign volunteers crowded around television sets. As newscasters reported the election results, the campaign workers cheered the addition of each new state to Clinton's total. When it was announced that Clinton's electoral votes had passed 270 — the number needed for election — the roar of the crowd outside echoed with the University of Arkansas hog-call rallying cry, "Woo! Pig! Sooey!"

Clinton's race for the White House had resulted in an amazing victory. At the beginning of his long struggle, in the chilly towns of New Hampshire, the odds were stacked against him. But Clinton survived by refusing to give up. Throughout the hard-fought campaign, he focused on the economic needs of the Americans he often called "the forgotten middle class."

Opposite page: Election night, 1992

Hillary Rodham Clinton, Bill Clinton, Al Gore, and Tipper Gore (left to right) greet the jubilant Little Rock crowd on election night.

On a platform erected outside the Arkansas statehouse, Vice-President-elect Al Gore and his family joined Clinton, his wife Hillary, and their daughter, Chelsea. Standing together in victory, they once again presented the image of youth and energy they had projected throughout the campaign.

Stepping to the microphone, President-elect Clinton began his victory speech: "My fellow Americans," he exclaimed, "on this day, with high hopes and brave hearts, in massive numbers the American people have voted to make a new beginning. This election is a clarion call for our country to face the challenges of the end of the Cold War and the beginning of the next century. To restore growth to our country and opportunity to our people . . . I

The new president and vice-president

accept, tonight, the responsibility that you have given me
to be the leader of this, the greatest country in human
history. I accept it with a full heart and a joyous spirit. But
I ask you to be Americans again, too. To be interested not
just in getting, but in giving . . . not just in looking out for
yourselves, but in looking out for others too . . . We're all
in this together and we will rise or fall together. That has
been my message to the American people for the past thirteen months and it will be my message for the next four
years. Together we can do it. Together we can make the
country that we love everything it was meant to be.''

To his supporters, Clinton represented a fresh start for
America. Forty-six-year-old Clinton would be the first
American president born after World War II.

Chapter 2

A Place Called Hope

On a rainy night in May 1946 an automobile sped along Highway 61 near Sikeston, Missouri. William Jefferson Blythe III, a young auto-parts salesman, drove through the darkness toward Hope, Arkansas. He was making a surprise visit home to see his pregnant wife, Virginia. Suddenly the car blew a tire and skidded off the road. The crash hurled Blythe from the car, and he was killed.

A few months later, on August 19, 1946, Virginia Cassidy Blythe gave birth to a healthy baby boy. She named the infant William Jefferson Blythe IV, after his dead father. Years later, when Bill Clinton had grown into a man, he would still say with regret, "I never met my father."

When her little son was two years old, Virginia Blythe decided to study nursing at Charity Hospital in New Orleans. Virginia realized she needed an education in nursing to support her son. Tearfully she made the sacrifice of being apart from him in those early years. Bill recalled visiting his mother in New Orleans. "I can still see her clearly . . . through the eyes of a three-year-old, kneeling at the railroad station and weeping as she put me back on the train to Arkansas."

The Hope, Arkansas, house where Billy lived with his grandparents

Billy stayed in Hope with his grandparents Eldridge and Edith Cassidy. Hope was a rural farming community in southwestern Arkansas. "For four years I lived with my grandparents," Bill Clinton remembered. "They didn't have much money. Nobody did in Arkansas at the end of World War II." There was no indoor plumbing in the Cassidy house.

Billy's loving grandparents taught him to read and count. "When I was three years old," he recalled, "they would sit me up in the high chair at breakfast and tack playing cards on the baseboards of the windows and make me count, and teach me to read, to add and subtract."

Toddler Billy

"You have got to do this," his grandfather said. "You have to learn these things so you can do better than I've done."

Eldridge Cassidy owned a small grocery store in a mostly black neighborhood in Hope. Little Billy learned by his grandfather's example how to treat all people with kindness and respect. Mr. Cassidy often extended credit to his customers. He knew they needed food even if they could not pay just then. That good-hearted lesson was not lost on the young boy helping out in his grandfather's shop. "He was the kindest person I ever knew," Bill later remembered. "Before I was big enough to see over the counter, I learned from him to look up to people other folks looked down upon."

Billy and a friend pose with their kindergarten teacher, Mary Perkins, in 1952.

Blue-eyed Billy Blythe grew into a smiling, cheerful boy. When he was four years old, he went to a local kindergarten run by Mary and Nannie Perkins. Classmate Joseph Purvis recalled that "one day . . . we were all playing high jump with a jump rope . . . during lunch recess . . . Two boys each [grabbed] an end of the rope, stretching it straight across." When it was Billy's turn to jump over the rope, his heel got caught and he fell hard to the ground. "I remember Bill wouldn't stop crying, and Miss Mary or Miss Nannie had to call his grandparents . . . Imagine my shock when I got home from school and found out that the reason Bill had been crying was that the fall broke his leg in three places."

Billy's grandfather carried him to the hospital. For many days, Billy lay with his leg suspended in the air and a plaster cast up to his hip.

BROOKWOOD

GRADE 1

1952 - 1953

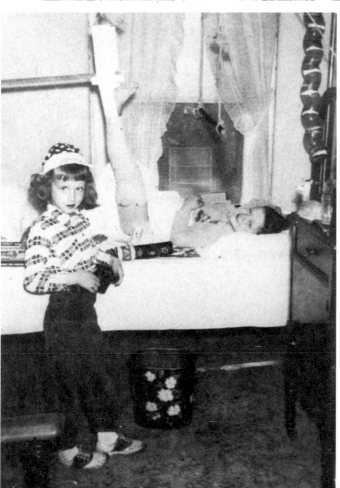

Top: Billy (top row, second from left) and his first-grade classmates
Bottom: Billy Clinton endures the pain of a broken leg with a smile on his face.

15

During that year, Virginia Blythe married Roger Clinton, a car salesman at his brother's Buick dealership in Hot Springs. Billy's new stepfather bought a farm for the family near Hot Springs, Arkansas. Billy never forgot one childhood experience there. "When I was seven or eight, a ram butted me and cut my head open . . . It was the awfullest beating I ever took and I had to go to the hospital for stitches." Nevertheless, Billy enjoyed outdoor life in the country.

Virginia Clinton sent her handsome, curly-haired little boy to a private Catholic grade school. At St. John's Catholic School in Hot Springs he soon became known as Billy Clinton. Seven-year-old Billy was so intelligent and alert that he answered questions before the other children could even raise their hands. "He started reading the newspaper in the first grade," his mother proudly recalled. Soon Billy developed a strong interest in current events. In 1955 Roger Clinton bought a black-and-white television set. Billy sat and watched the 1956 Democratic National Convention on television and quickly became fascinated with politics.

Bill entered the Ramble School, a public elementary school in Hot Springs, when he reached fourth grade. According to his boyhood friend David Leopoulos, "Bill used a catchphrase, 'Hot Dog!' Every time he would get excited about something, he would use that phrase. In less than a week most everyone in the school was saying 'Hot Dog!' I never knew anyone who did not like Bill, for he treated everyone with respect."

When Bill was ten, his mother and stepfather had a son, whom they named Roger, Jr. Virginia Clinton still worked hard as a nurse anesthetist. Many times hospital duty kept her from home, and as he grew older, Bill often helped by baby-sitting little Roger.

Unfortunately, the Clinton home was not always a happy place. Roger Clinton suffered from alcoholism. He was usually calm, but when he drank, he sometimes erupted with anger. There were frequent arguments between Virginia and Roger, and sometimes he slapped and punched her. During one of his worst rages, he fired a gun into the living room wall and was put in jail.

The many fights that Bill witnessed at home upset him deeply. One day, he had simply had enough. "One of the most difficult things for me was being fourteen and putting an end to the violence," he said later. "I just broke down the door of their room one night when they were having an encounter and told him that I was bigger than him now, and there would never be any more of this while I was there." He took his mother and his younger half-brother by the hand and issued a hard warning to his stepfather: "You will never hit either of them again. If you want them, you'll have to go through me." Though Roger Clinton's drinking continued, the violence ended.

Virginia and Roger Clinton divorced when Bill was fourteen. Three months later, though, Roger convinced Virginia that he could stop drinking. Virginia still loved Roger, and she remarried him. Bill made the best of it, and to make his mother happy, he legally changed his last name. In 1960, teenaged Bill Blythe became Bill Clinton.

Although his stepfather drank, Bill really cared for him: "He was a wonderful person, but he didn't like himself very much . . . It really was a painful experience to see someone you love . . . that you care about, just in the grip of a demon . . . I had a good normal life, but at times it was really tough. I had to learn to live with the darker side of life at a fairly early period."

Bill's mother remained perhaps the most important influence in his life. While he was in high school, the two often discussed the pressing moral issues of the times. After a long day at the hospital, she sometimes rushed into the kitchen muttering. "It's just not fair." Together, mother and son endlessly discussed the world's many social problems.

Classmate Carolyn Yeldell Staley talked about the Clintons' home at 213 Scully Street. "Above the carport was a basketball goal which Bill spent many hours enjoying. He loved to shoot baskets with friends or by himself . . . The time we spent together was often either at my house or Bill's, listening to music, playing and singing at the piano, and reading . . . Bill was always reading something."

At Hot Springs High School Bill was an excellent student and always got high grades. "At fifteen, Bill was already . . . a tall, gangly kid with an ever-present smile and an intense interest in everything," said history teacher Paul Root. Bill's interests included student theater, where he played leading roles in *Arsenic and Old Lace* and other productions. He became president of the Beta Club (for outstanding academic achievement) and joined the math club, the Latin club, and the science club.

Bill Clinton, the busy high school student: he was a standout saxophone player in the school band (right), and he also won several academic awards (at left, he poses with a co-winner of the local Elks Youth Leadership Award).

"His band activities took up a lot of time," recalled David Leopoulos. "He really got into his music." Bill spent hours practicing his tenor saxophone. He played in the marching band, concert band, stage band, pep band, band key club, and combos. His talent eventually won him first chair tenor saxophone in the All-State First Band, the highest honor a high-school musician could earn.

"Cool" Bill (center) and his bandmates: The Three Kings.

Schoolmate Randy Goodrum joined Bill Clinton and Joe Newman in forming an instrumental trio called The Three Kings. "We rehearsed wherever we could gather around a piano," recalled Goodrum. "During that two-year period I got to know Bill quite well. He had the extraordinary ability to give you 100 percent of his attention when you talked or worked with him. He had an amazing memory, was a great listener, and even though he was the leader of the band, he would take any and all suggestions and use them if they made sense—sometimes while we were on stage."

Bill Clinton spread himself thin during his high-school years. As his guidance counselor Edith Irons later

Even as a teenager, Bill was devoted to the Democratic party: pinned to his collar is a Kennedy-Johnson campaign button.

observed, "I don't know how he could be on the band field at 6 A.M. and be back at school and go, go, go all day."

Always interested in politics, Bill served on the high-school student council. He also involved himself in many community services such as the Kiwanis Key Club and the Elks Club. The early 1960s filled many Americans with idealism. President John F. Kennedy's speeches thrilled people with the zest and the youthful spirit of his "New Frontier" politics. "I decided to be a Democrat," Clinton later explained, "starting in the presidential election of 1960, when John Kennedy excited me with a promise to get the country moving again. I think he gave people the sense that they could make a difference."

In the summer of 1963, sixteen-year-old Clinton took part in Boys' State, a program run by the American Legion to teach young leaders about government and politics. Bill ran for Boys' State senator, shaking hands and passing out leaflets among the more than 1,000 kids who crammed into the Boys' State camp barracks. His election prize was a trip to Washington, D.C., as an Arkansas delegate to the national convention of Boys' Nation. In Washington he enjoyed lunching in the Senate Dining Room with Arkansas senator J. William Fulbright. Even more exciting, on a sunny afternoon in July, he and other Boys' State senators trooped into the Rose Garden at the White House. There, Bill Clinton shook hands with President Kennedy. "I'd never seen him get so excited about something," exclaimed Virginia. "When he came back from Washington, holding this picture of himself with Jack Kennedy, and the expression on his face . . . I knew right then that politics was the answer for him."

Sadly, less than four months later, on November 22, 1963, an assassin's bullet killed Kennedy in Dallas, Texas. For a week the flag at Hot Springs High School flew at half-mast. Along with millions of other Americans, Clinton mourned the tragic death of the president. His friend David Leopoulos recalled, "We were all crushed when we lost our leader." Bill Clinton felt an even greater desire to try to make a difference in the Kennedy tradition.

"By the time I was seventeen," he said later, "I knew that if I was in school in Washington I would have many opportunities to learn a lot about foreign affairs, domestic politics, and economics." Without hesitation he applied to

An incredible moment: the future president meets President Kennedy in 1963.

attend college at Georgetown University's School of Foreign Service.

Clinton graduated from Hot Springs High in 1964, finishing fourth in a class of more than three hundred. He looked forward to going away to college, enjoying some real independence, and finding out what he wanted to do with his life. More than anything he wanted to get involved in public service and politics.

Clinton's high-school
yearbook (senior-year
photo, left) reveals the
variety of his extra-
curricular activities. He was
involved in school politics,
music, theater, and sports.

● CHRISTOPHER, George H. — Thespians 3.
● CLEMONS, Lloyd — Football 1,2,3, Letterman 2.3,
● CLINTON, William J. — Boys State 2; Boys Nation
2; Junior Class President 2; National Merit Scholarship
Semifinalist 2; Academically Talented Student Award 2;
Beta Club 1,2,3, President 3; Mu Alpha Theta 1,2,3,
Vice-President 2; Junior Classical League 1,2, President
2; Bio Chem Phy 2,3; Key Club 2,3; Student Council
2,3; ARSENIC AND OLD LACE 2; Trojan Band 1,2,3,
Major 3; First Chair All State Band 2.

**Above: Hot Springs High School's National Merit Semifinalists
(Clinton is second from right)
Below: Bill shows his theatrical side as emcee of his high school's talent show.**

Chapter 3

Student With a Conscience

Great changes were taking place in the United States in 1964. On June 29, shortly after Bill's acceptance to Georgetown, the important Civil Rights Bill of 1964 became law. On August 7, Congress passed the Gulf of Tonkin resolution, giving President Lyndon Johnson power to take greater military action in Vietnam. Meanwhile, the music of the Beatles was sweeping the nation, signaling the birth of many new cultural trends.

That fall, Bill Clinton, with his brown hair cut short, entered Georgetown University. Worried about paying his school expenses, he telephoned Senator Fulbright's office in search of a job. Lee Williams, chief assistant to the senator, explained, "We don't have a full-time job, but we do have two part-time slots open." One paid $5,000 per year and the other $3,500 per year. "I'll take 'em both," Clinton responded. "You're just the guy I'm looking for," said Williams.

And so Clinton started working for Senator William Fulbright, chairman of the Senate Foreign Relations Committee. In the mailroom of Fulbright's office, Clinton opened sacks of mail about Vietnam and other political issues.

President of his freshman class at Georgetown University, Bill wrote the summary of the academic year for the yearbook.

At Georgetown, Clinton worked for a bachelor of arts degree, majoring in international government studies. Classmate Dru Bachman remembered, "Everyone at Georgetown knew of Bill Clinton . . . He openly admitted to being a small-town boy who had come to the big city to soak up every ounce of information and experience he could find."

Early in the school year, Clinton ran for president of the freshman class. "You must know the rules before you can change them," he proclaimed after winning that election. Clinton's sophomore year found him once again president of his class. Student affairs and national government seemed to fill his mind. Roommate Chris Ashby recollected, "We talked nightly, and sometimes into the night, about what was going on in the city and in the world."

Every weekend, Bill drove more than two hundred miles to be with his stepfather, who was dying of cancer. Roger Clinton was at Duke University Medical Center in North Carolina. As he grew older, Bill had begun to understand his stepfather's alcoholic addiction. One Easter weekend, he and his stepfather attended a service at the Duke chapel. "It was beautiful," Bill recalled. "I think he knew that I was coming down there just because I loved him. There was nothing else to fight over, nothing else to run from." Later that year, Roger Clinton died.

The Vietnam War brought sadness into many American lives during Clinton's years at Georgetown. On the wire-service printer at work, Bill noted the names, ages, and hometowns of hundreds of people killed in Vietnam. He identified those from Arkansas so that Senator Fulbright could send a personal letter of sympathy to each family.

Martin Luther King's assassination by James Earl Ray in Memphis, Tennessee, on April 4, 1968, triggered the worst race riots in U.S. history. For Bill Clinton, Martin Luther King had been a hero. He admired King's leadership, moral courage, and idealism in his struggle for civil rights. After King was murdered, Bill stood on the roof of his Georgetown dormitory and watched neighborhoods burn in the city of Washington. To ease the suffering in needy areas Clinton slapped a Red Cross sign on the side of his white Buick convertible and loaded groceries into the trunk. Bill's old friend Carolyn Staley helped him. "We delivered our boxes of supplies to the basement of a church," she remembered, "where people were staying who were homeless because of the fires and damage."

As a Georgetown
senior

Clinton's top grades earned him a chance to apply for a Rhodes scholarship in his senior year. Rhodes scholarships enable a select group of scholastic achievers to pursue advanced university studies at Oxford University in England. Bill's mother sat by the phone all day, waiting for him to call with the news of the Rhodes committee's decision. When he finally phoned, he cheerfully asked, "Well, Mother, how do you think I'll look in English tweed?" He had won a scholarship.

In the fall of 1968, thirty-two Rhodes scholars stepped aboard the SS *United States* in New York City. Bill Clinton joined America's top students on deck as the ship set sail for England. Clinton was enrolled at Oxford's University College, where he would study for a graduate degree in politics.

Oxford University, England

Clinton now stood six feet two inches tall and weighed nearly 230 pounds. "Bill . . . towered over Oxford undergraduates," fellow student John Isaacson remembered. "He greeted every reluctant, shy, perfectly mannered English schoolboy with a big grin, a hearty handshake, and a serious dose of down-home Americana. Some of them have never recovered." American Rhodes Scholar Tom Williamson recalled, "We would hitchhike to London on weekends to sample English theater."

Often Clinton and his friends at Oxford stayed up late at night debating important issues of the day. As the Vietnam War dragged on, many Americans began to question U.S. involvement. Protesters in the United States were staging large-scale demonstrations against the war. At Oxford, Clinton joined the antiwar movement, even helping to organize rallies and protests.

In 1969, Clinton received his own U.S. military draft notice. To avoid going immediately into the army, he arranged to join the Army Reserve Officer Training Corps (ROTC) program at the University of Arkansas Law School in Fayetteville. Sometime in October, though, he decided to make himself available for the draft. By October 30, the draft board placed Bill Clinton in the 1-A category—completely qualified to serve.

All that remained between Bill Clinton and military service in Vietnam was the draft lottery. On December 1, 1969, Clinton received his lottery number—311. It was high enough to assure him that he would never be called into service.

Returning to the United States from Oxford, Clinton obtained a scholarship to Yale Law School in New Haven, Connecticut, for the fall of 1970. To pay his living expenses, he found a number of part-time jobs. He worked for a lawyer in downtown New Haven, assisted a city politician in Hartford, and even taught at a nearby community college. His first semester, though, was spent as a volunteer in Connecticut politician Joe Duffy's unsuccessful attempt to win a U.S. Senate seat. Clinton worked the phones from morning to night, talking with voters. It was

Yale Law School,
in New Haven,
Connecticut

an old-fashioned campaign, with town meetings and door-to-door visits, and Clinton loved every minute of it.

After that election campaign, Clinton returned to his Yale Law School studies. Roommate Don Pogue remembered, "Bill worked hard . . . He would always take his papers back and rewrite them one last time."

As a proud Arkansan, Clinton spent hours in the student lounge telling his friends tales about his hometowns of Hope and Hot Springs. One day, a young law student named Hillary Rodham passed through the lounge with some classmates. She overheard a loud voice declare, "And not only that, we have the largest watermelons in the world!" When she asked her friends who the speaker was, they replied, "Oh, that's Bill Clinton, and all he ever talks about is Arkansas."

Several days later, Clinton stood chatting with a student at the Yale Law School library. As he talked, he noticed a blonde young woman at the far end of the room. "She was down at the other end," he recalled, "and . . . I just was staring at her . . . She closed this book, and she walked all the way down the library . . . and she came up to me and she said, 'Look, if you're going to keep staring at me, and I'm going to keep staring back, I think we should at least know each other. I'm Hillary Rodham. What's your name?' "

Born into a wealthy family in Chicago on October 26, 1947, Hillary Rodham had grown up in the suburb of Park Ridge. She attended Wellesley College in Massachusetts, and entered Yale Law School in 1970. After meeting Bill Clinton, she began dating him regularly.

Though Clinton did very well at his law school studies, he was actually more interested in politics than in law. In the summer and fall of 1972, Bill Clinton and Hillary Rodham decided to go to Texas as volunteers in Senator George McGovern's Democratic presidential campaign. Hillary worked in San Antonio registering Hispanic voters, while Bill helped run the Texas Democratic campaign headquarters in Austin. Clinton and Rodham spent the entire semester working in Texas, and then returned to Yale in time for their final exams. The two brilliant students, who had not attended a single class, passed their finals easily.

While at Yale, Clinton and Rodham became partners in the law school's annual trial competition. According to student Douglas Eakeley, Rodham's legal skills were a perfect

Early in his political career, Bill Clinton worked for the 1972 McGovern presidential campaign. Here he greets Senator McGovern (center) at the Little Rock airport.

match with Clinton's. "Hillary has the same wonderful personal warmth and commitment to public service that Bill has. But coming from the Middle West, she was more direct and outspoken than Bill, the gentle Southerner. They made a wonderful team."

Many of Clinton's Yale classmates looked forward to high-paying jobs at major law firms, but not twenty-six-year-old Bill Clinton. He had decided to serve the people of his poor home state in whatever way he could. Upon graduation, Clinton packed his bags and boxes, got into his car, and headed home for Arkansas.

"All I wanted to do was go home," he explained. "I thought I would hang out my shingle in Hot Springs and see if I could run for office."

Chapter 4

Young Man in a Hurry

Bill Clinton planned to establish a small-town Arkansas law practice. One of his Yale professors, however, told him of two openings at the University of Arkansas Law School in Fayetteville. Driving home to Hot Springs, Clinton stopped at a telephone booth and called about the jobs. "I don't have anything set to do," he told Arkansas Law School official Wylie Davis, "but I'm coming home to Arkansas, and you might want me to come teach up there a year because I'll teach anything, and I don't mind working."

Clinton was quickly offered a teaching appointment, and the fall of 1973 found Professor Bill Clinton striding across the campus of the University of Arkansas. Law student Luther Hardin recalled, "My memory of Bill Clinton is that of a teacher who was comfortable in the classroom . . . and enjoyed teaching."

Politics still held Clinton's greatest interest, however. In early 1974, just six months out of law school, Clinton decided to run against John Paul Hammerschmidt, the popular Republican congressman from Arkansas' Third Congressional District. Clinton knew it would be an uphill battle and he did not expect to win. "The only reason I ran for Congress is they couldn't get anybody else to do it," he later claimed. "I [hadn't planned] to get into politics that early. I was sort of easing into my life."

"When Bill ran for Congress in 1974," Professor Ann Rainwater Henry remembered, "his boundless energy and enthusiasm were contagious. He inspired us all and we became involved with his campaign in fund-raising, phone-calling, working at headquarters—whatever our schedules would allow us to do." Clinton drove his car thousands of miles back and forth across the Third Congressional District. His speeches called for a fairer tax system, a national health insurance program, and public funding of presidential elections.

With skill and effort Clinton won the Democratic primary. Next he focused on beating Hammerschmidt in the general election. "We need a congressman," he explained during his campaign, "who's not afraid to say no to the unnecessary government spending that has hurt the economy of the country . . . We ought to go back to the roots of our democracy—the people. They have some ideas of their own about what the politicians ought to do."

In the fall 1974 election, Clinton almost defeated John Paul Hammerschmidt. He earned 48.2 percent of the vote and won thirteen of twenty-one counties. Although he lost the election, he impressed many voters. A report in the *Arkansas Gazette* noted that "Bill Clinton very nearly made it to Congress and surely he will be back in 1976."

While Clinton campaigned for Congress, Hillary Rodham was working in Washington, D.C., for the House Judiciary Committee. That committee was responsible for planning the impeachment trial of President Richard Nixon following the Watergate scandal. When President Nixon resigned in August 1974, Hillary Rodham moved down to Arkansas to teach at the University of Arkansas Law School. She and Bill Clinton quickly resumed their blossoming romance.

One day in August 1975, a year after arriving in Fayetteville, Hillary returned from an out-of-town trip. "Bill picked me up," she recalled, "but instead of driving me to my apartment, he drove me up to this house, and he said, 'I've bought that house you like.'

'What house I like?' I asked.

'You know,' he said. 'Remember when we were driving around the day before you left and there was a For Sale sign and you said, 'Gee, that's a nice house'?

'Bill, that's all I said. I've never been inside it.'

'Well, I thought you liked it, so I bought it,' he said. 'So I guess we'll have to get married now.' "

Bill and Hillary decided they wanted to be married in that house on California Drive. So, with brushes, buckets, and ladders, Clinton and his friends rushed to paint the house, inside and out, in time for the wedding. On October 11, 1975, the loving couple exchanged rings in a private wedding ceremony.

Hillary Rodham Clinton in 1975

Both newlyweds continued teaching law at the University of Arkansas in Fayetteville. Clinton taught one college class on the Arkansas criminal code during the spring 1976 term. The course prepared him for his next job—attorney general of Arkansas. Clinton officially filed as a candidate on April 1, 1976. In November 1976 the thirty-year-old law professor triumphed over two opponents in the Democratic primary. Since no Republicans had filed for the position, Clinton won the general election automatically.

Deputy Attorney General Joseph Purvis remembered, "Bill quickly instilled a feeling among everyone who worked in the office that we were on a mission to work for the public." During his two-year term as attorney general, Clinton fulfilled a campaign promise to expand work-release programs for prisoners in order to reduce prison overcrowding. In addition, the *Arkansas Gazette* praised Attorney General Clinton for being "a stout champion of the Arkansas consumer."

For some time now, Clinton had had his sights set on the governorship. He felt the need to improve economic and social conditions in Arkansas, which ranked among the neediest states in the nation.

"One day," his friend David Matthews recalled, "we were discussing whether he should run for the United States Senate or for governor." "I believe I can do more good for the people of Arkansas as governor," Clinton decided.

In the 1978 Democratic primary race, Clinton ran for governor and captured 59.4 percent of the vote. In the general election, he faced Republican state chairman Lynn Lowe. In his speeches Clinton stressed that Arkansas' economic problems could be helped only by improving the quality of education in the state. He noted, however, that it was extremely difficult to improve education in a state where teachers were paid less than anywhere else in the United States. Arkansas citizens seemed to agree. The Arkadelphia *Southern Standard* correctly guessed at Clinton's chances: "He cannot lose unless he stumbles badly." On election day 1978, Clinton received 338,684 votes—63.4 percent of the total.

Newly elected Governor Clinton meets President Carter in December 1978.

Thirty-two-year-old Bill Clinton had come a long way. He was the second-youngest governor in the history of the United States. National news programs and magazines called him Arkansas' Boy Governor.

On January 9, 1979, Clinton took the oath as the fortieth governor of Arkansas. "For as long as I can remember," he stated in his inaugural address, "I have believed [deeply] in the cause of equal opportunity, and I will do what I can to advance it . . . For as long as I can remember, I have wished to ease the burdens of life for those who,

The second-youngest governor in the nation's history takes the oath of office in 1979.

through no fault of their own, are old or weak or needy, and I will do what I can to help them . . . We are a people of pride and hope, of vision and will . . . We have an opportunity to forge a future that is more remarkable, rich, and fulfilling to all Arkansans than our proud past. We must not squander it. There is much to be done."

"When he began his administration in 1979," remarked his friend David Matthews, "Bill was like a man in a hurry to accomplish many things in a short time."

As governor, Clinton made immediate efforts in the area he cared most about—education. Arkansas ranked last among the fifty states in education. Clinton's first state budget called for a huge increase in spending for public schooling. The budget included a $1,200 salary increase for teachers. Clinton won approval for a statewide educational testing program that would measure student performance in the basic subjects. He also pushed forward a law requiring that all teachers take the national teacher's examination before they could be certified to teach in Arkansas. In addition, under the governor's leadership, the state set up a summer school for talented children from across Arkansas.

At the outset of his two-year term, Clinton also promised a new law raising motor vehicle registration fees. This "car tag" fee was intended to provide money for a major Arkansas highway-repair program. Many people complained about this new tax, however.

On February 27, 1980, the Clintons' daughter, Chelsea, was born. As Clinton neared the end of his term, a problem erupted in Arkansas that no one could have foreseen. In the spring of 1980, thousands of political refugees flooded into the United States from Cuba. President Jimmy Carter decided to house nearly 20,000 of these Cuban "boat-lift" people at Fort Chaffee, a federal army base in Arkansas. Rough living conditions at Fort Chaffee upset many of the refugees. On May 26, 1980, some three hundred unruly Cubans crashed through barricades and escaped through the fort's unguarded gate, roaming across the countryside. Clinton reacted quickly and forcefully. He

Rising in national prominence, Governor Clinton discusses the issues with NBC's Tom Brokaw.

ordered National Guard troops to protect Arkansas citizens living near Fort Chaffee. Within three days, all of the Cubans had been recaptured by local and state police officers.

Four days later, however, Fort Chaffee exploded into a full-blown riot. The press called it a war zone. Angry Cubans charged the gate. About two hundred of them ran down Arkansas Highway 22, toward the small community of Barling. Just outside the town, policemen wielding nightsticks managed to turn them back.

Cuban refugees at Fort Chaffee noted in 1980; this prison revolt marred the final days of Clinton's first term as governor.

On the phone to Washington, Clinton sternly told White House officials, "Listen, you can do two things. You can come down here and fix this tonight, right now, or I'm going to call out the entire National Guard and shut the place down." On June 2, the White House finally ordered federal troops to keep the Cubans from leaving Fort Chaffee. The *Hot Springs News* praised Clinton for his role in managing the crisis: "All Arkansans should be grateful to Governor Clinton for . . . finally forcing Jimmy Carter to stop tending his roses and start tending to the safety of the people."

But the Fort Chaffee riots hurt Clinton's chances for reelection nonetheless. Frank White, the Republican candidate for governor, scolded Clinton for not standing up to

The governor answers tough questions.

President Carter sooner during the crisis. He also attacked Clinton for his automobile tax increases. White coined a slogan that his supporters chanted throughout the state: "Cubans and Car Tags."

On election night 1980, thirty-four-year-old Bill Clinton admitted defeat to Frank White. He had lost by only 35,000 votes out of 840,000 cast. The morning after the election, the young governor appeared on the steps of the State Capitol. "Hillary and I have shed a few tears for our loss of last evening," he said, "but we accept the will of [the] people." As Clinton left office, the *Arkansas Gazette* commented, "It is sad to see Clinton go . . . [he] has learned lessons that will serve him in the future."

Chapter 5

The Comeback Kid

As the youngest ex-governor in the history of the United States, Clinton had a lot of time on his hands. He soon joined the Little Rock law firm of Wright Lindsey & Jennings and began planning his return to politics.

"When I decided I didn't want to give up and I wanted to go on in politics," he said, "I realized I had to be in better communication with the voters. I began to drive around the state and talk to people." For the last six months of 1981, he crisscrossed the state, apologizing to Arkansans for not listening enough to their problems and complaints.

In February 1982, Clinton took to the airwaves with a paid television advertisement announcing his candidacy for governor. He admitted that he had made some mistakes but promised that he had learned from them. Clinton's campaign slogan revealed his new attitude about governing: "You can't lead without listening."

The *Arkansas Gazette* endorsed Clinton, praising his "ability to bring the ideas and leadership the state so desperately needs." That newspaper also noted that "Mrs. Clinton is almost certainly the best speaker among politicians' wives, probably the only one who can fully engage an audience on her own merits."

Opposite page: The Clintons are a powerful political team.

Hillary Rodham Clinton worked as a senior partner with a Little Rock law firm. She also served as chairwoman of a national youth health and welfare organization called the Children's Defense Fund.

For months, Democrat Bill Clinton and Republican Frank White battled in a bitter campaign. Finally, with 54.7 percent of the vote, Clinton defeated White in the fall 1982 election. He was the first Arkansas ex-governor ever to be returned to the statehouse.

Clinton's inauguration speech in January 1983 focused on education and other critical issues facing Arkansas. Soon Governor Clinton appointed his wife, Hillary Rodham Clinton, to chair the state's new Arkansas Education Standards Committee. Hillary traveled all over the state holding hearings and meeting with parents and teachers. In the end, her committee submitted a plan for drastic changes in the state's education system.

Arkansas turned on their television sets to hear Governor Clinton speak on September 19, 1983. "My fellow Arkansans," he began, "I want to talk to you tonight about the real problems we have in education. They are costing us jobs today and damaging our future. To put it bluntly, we've got to raise taxes to increase your investment in education. Arkansas is dead last in spending per child."

Across the state Clinton went on the stump, whipping up support for his education program. The governor told the *Arkansas Gazette* that improving the education system was "more important to me than anything I have ever done in politics."

Governor-elect Clinton talks to the press after winning his second-term election.

In town meetings all over Arkansas, Clinton asked people to pay higher taxes so that the young people of Arkansas could have a better education. At the State Capitol in Little Rock, Clinton worked hard to get his proposals passed. He served as his own lobbyist, calling legislators at all hours of the night and wandering through the halls of the statehouse armed with a notepad and a cup of coffee. At last, at the end of 1983, the legislature raised taxes to improve education in Arkansas.

During Clinton's second term, an event occurred that deeply affected the governor. In May 1984, Clinton received a telephone call from Colonel Tommy Goodwin, director of the Arkansas State Police. Goodwin revealed that Clinton's brother, Roger, was under investigation for selling cocaine. Clinton was stunned. "What do you want us to do?" Goodwin asked. "Do what you'd normally do," Clinton replied with a heavy heart.

Three months later, the police arrested Roger in Hot Springs. After his brother was taken into custody, Governor Clinton announced, "This is a time of great pain and sadness for me and my family. My brother has apparently become involved with drugs, a curse which . . . has plagued the lives of millions of families in our nation . . . I love my brother very much and will be of comfort to him, but I want his case to be handled exactly as any other similar case would be."

In November, Roger was sent to prison for two years. After Roger's sentencing, Governor Clinton told the press, "I accept the judgment of the court with respect. Now all of us in my brother's family must do everything we can to help him free himself of his drug dependency . . . I am more deeply committed than ever before to all that I can do to fight against illegal drugs and to prevent other families from experiencing the personal tragedy and pain drug abuse has brought to us."

After his release, Roger began giving numerous talks about the dangers of drug abuse to children across Arkansas. He wished to help young people avoid the terrible mistake he had made.

Clinton discusses public education on the "Donahue" show in 1985.

Despite the publicity over his brother's addiction, Clinton remained a popular figure in Arkansas due to his successes as governor. He entered his 1984 reelection campaign full of hope, and he ended up winning easily, with 63 percent of the vote.

Clinton seemed confident when he took office in January 1985. In this third inaugural address, he promised to make state job growth as important as his effort to improve state education. "We must believe in ourselves and our ability to shape our own destiny," he declared. "The future need not be fate; it can be achievement."

During his third term, Governor Clinton signed a law requiring speedy trials and another protecting the rights of crime victims. On March 23, 1985, teachers across Arkansas took the nation's first basic skills test for classroom teachers.

On his 1985 trade mission to Japan, Clinton met with Shizuya Inaba, an Osaka, Japan, industry leader.

By the mid-1980s, Bill Clinton was becoming a national figure. In May 1985, he told the *Atlanta Constitution,* "It would be fun to run [for president], even if you lost. It would be a challenge to go out and meet the people and try to communicate your ideas and bring the different parts of the country together." At the end of the year, he led an international trade delegation from Arkansas to Japan, where he received a warm welcome.

In the summer of 1986, Clinton served as the co-chairman of the National Governors Association task force on welfare reform. "Can we make America work again for her people?" he asked. "I believe we can, but only if we find ways for Americans to be able to work and have work." Clinton insisted that welfare programs should be job programs. Applying that belief in Arkansas, the gover-

Daughter Chelsea (age 6) exits a voting booth with her father in 1986; Clinton was reelected to a fourth term as Arkansas' governor.

nor set up a program that, by 1991, was helping over 200 people per month move from the welfare rolls to the work force.

An impressive 64 percent of Arkansas voters returned Clinton to a fourth term as governor in 1986. That election marked the first time in more than 100 years that the governor's term would be four years rather than two. (In 1984, Arkansas voters had approved a state constitutional amendment lengthening the governor's term of office.)

In his victory speech on election day, Clinton said, "In our 150th year, I believe with all my heart our best years are ahead of us. The tough campaign is over and now it's time for the hard work to begin on our problems and our opportunities. It's time for all of us to pull together as a family."

As Clinton's popularity grew, some politicians predicted that he might one day be a presidential candidate. Clinton saw a chance to increase his national profile when he nominated Governor Michael Dukakis of Massachusetts for president at the 1988 Democratic National Convention in Atlanta, Georgia. Instead, he managed to embarrass himself. At the last minute, Dukakis's political advisers insisted that Clinton use the speech they had written for him. Clinton did the best he could, but his 33-minute speech seemed endless. The only applause he got was when he finally said, "In conclusion . . . ." NBC commentator John Chancellor noted, "I am afraid that . . . one of the most attractive governors just put a blot on his record." A few days later, Clinton regained some public appeal by playing his saxophone on the "Tonight Show" and by poking lighthearted fun at himself with host Johnny Carson.

Back at the Arkansas statehouse, Clinton succeeded in tightening enforcement of child support laws and in reforming the juvenile justice system. He signed a law providing for military-style "boot camps" instead of jail for first-time offenders. Clinton also worked hard getting his education reform package through the legislature.

No one except Bill and Hillary Clinton knew whether or not he would seek an unheard-of fifth term in office. Political advisers warned the governor that another term might harm his long-term national ambitions, but in early March 1990, he decided to run again. Clinton faced Republican Sheffield Nelson—a former Democrat—and in the end Clinton triumphed with 57 percent of the vote. "The people said they wanted Bill Clinton for four more

A rising star in the Democratic party, Clinton addressed the 1988 Democratic Convention in Atlanta, but the impression he made was not all good.

years," Nelson admitted in defeat, "and I don't think it would have made any difference who was against him. He was just that strong."

Governor Clinton opened his fifth term in January 1991 with a string of new proposals. He called for a new law requiring drivers under eighteen to show proof of school attendance, and asked that the school attendance age be raised from sixteen to seventeen.

Bill Clinton's leadership skills sparked admiration from his fellow governors. In a June 1991 poll, *Newsweek* magazine found that 39 percent of America's fifty governors—Democrats and Republicans alike—considered Bill Clinton to be the nation's most effective state executive.

Chapter 6

In the Race

The morning of October 3, 1991, dawned bright and clear. At noon that day, on the steps of the Old State House in Little Rock, Bill Clinton told a cheering crowd that he had decided to run for president of the United States.

For twelve years, Republicans Ronald Reagan (1981-89) and George Bush (took office in 1989) had held the White House. During Bush's presidency, unemployment had soared and many banks had failed. Americans were worried about the huge national debt created during the Republican administrations. Many Democrats believed George Bush could be beaten if only they had the right candidate.

In his announcement, Bill Clinton promised to turn the country around. He said, "Make no mistake. This election is about change.... This is not just a campaign for the presidency—it is a campaign for the future."

Full of energy, Bill Clinton set out on the long road to win the Democratic nomination. He was a long shot. Five other Democrats also joined the race. Several were better known than Bill Clinton and better acquainted with how things worked in Washington, D.C.

Five of the six Democratic candidates for president: Jerry Brown, Bill Clinton, Tom Harkin, Bob Kerry, and Paul Tsongas (left to right).

The first primary was scheduled for New Hampshire. A group of Clinton's longtime friends went there to help him campaign. They became known as the Arkansas Travelers. These dozens of loyal friends and admirers crisscrossed the state. They shook hands, passed out leaflets, and held town meetings on behalf of Bill Clinton, their "favorite son" candidate.

Clinton's campaign went well until a scandalous story broke in national newspapers in January 1992. An Arkansas woman named Gennifer Flowers claimed she'd been romantically involved with Clinton for twelve years. Clinton insisted the story was not true. He and his wife were interviewed on the television show "60 Minutes." In

On a morning jog in Little Rock, Clinton encounters an old friend.

that interview, Hillary Rodham Clinton said of her husband, "I'm sitting here because I love him and I respect him, and I honor what he's been through and what we've been through together. And you know, if that's not enough for people, then heck . . . don't vote for him."

Other stories came out claiming that Clinton had used influence to stay out of the military draft in 1969. Clinton was repeatedly forced to explain his past. In previous elections, candidates had quit under such pressure. But Clinton stayed in the race and concentrated on addressing issues of national concern.

His perseverance paid off. In the New Hampshire primary, he finished a strong second with 25 percent of the vote. A few weeks later, he won the Georgia primary. He then added stunning victories in Florida, Louisiana, Mississippi, Texas, Tennessee, and Missouri. "Bill Clinton's rise is . . . the story of a single-minded candidate with a strong sense of message," reported *Time* magazine. By June 1992, Clinton had clinched the Democratic nomination.

"It's been a long fight," Clinton said, reflecting on his victory. But the real struggle had just begun: the general election.

A huge groundswell of support had risen for H. Ross Perot, a self-made billionaire from Texas. In several television appearances, Perot had complained that none of the presidential candidates were capable of tackling the huge national debt. Perot's many supporters hit the streets petitioning for him, and finally won him a place on the ballot in every state.

By June, Perot's blunt, folksy style drew so much attention that many people forgot about Bill Clinton. Clinton sank in popularity. To boost his exposure, Clinton launched a television campaign. He appeared on all sorts of television programs, from news interviews to town hall meetings on MTV to a saxophone-playing stint on the "Arsenio Hall Show." Clinton won back his popularity by displaying a relaxed personality that appealed to younger voters. In July, he chose Senator Al Gore of Tennessee to be his vice-presidential running mate. If Clinton, age 45, and Gore, age 44, won the election, they would be the youngest pair ever to make it to the White House.

Excited Democrats gathered at their four-day national convention in July 1992. New York Governor Mario Cuomo officially nominated Clinton for president. "Step aside, Mr Bush," Cuomo said. "You've had your parade!"

Clinton plays his sax on "Arsenio Hall," June 4, 1992.

The crowd at Madison Square Garden erupted with glee as Bill Clinton stepped to the podium. He said, "In the name of all those who do the work, pay the taxes, raise the kids, and play by the rules...in the name of hardworking Americans who make up our forgotten middle class...I proudly accept your nomination for the presidency of the United States."

The Democrats left New York brimming with happy confidence. Clinton's nationally televised speech had struck a chord across the country. The next day, Ross Perot said that he felt the Democratic Party had "revitalized itself," so he pulled out of the race.

Always on the move: scenes of Clinton exercising (top) were a fixture of the campaign; after the Democratic convention, the Clintons and Gores embarked on a one-thousand-mile campaign trip by bus.

Chapter 7

The Final Lap

Bill Clinton's popularity zoomed after the convention. Instead of resting after the convention, Clinton and Gore set off on a bus trip from New York City to St. Louis. At stops along the 1,200-mile route they drew huge and enthusiastic crowds.

George Bush and Vice President Dan Quayle were nominated at the Republican National Convention in August. And on October 1, a month before the election, Ross Perot surprised everyone again by reentering the race.

The three presidential candidates met in a series of televised debates. Bill Clinton enjoyed this forum because he appeared so comfortable talking about the issues. Bush and Perot, however, continued attacking Clinton's character. George Bush repeatedly questioned Clinton's ability to be commander in chief of the nation's military because while he was a student in England, Clinton had protested against the Vietnam war, and he had avoided the military draft.

The attacks failed to slow Clinton's unstoppable rise in the polls. Clinton's call for change in government had won

In the last weeks before the election, the debates with Bush (right) and Perot (left) showed the nation that Clinton had a firm grasp on the most important issues.

over the American public. On Election Day, November 3, 1992, Americans walked into their polling places to cast their votes. The final results:

	Popular Votes	Electoral Votes
Bill Clinton	44,909,889	370
George Bush	39,104,545	168
Ross Perot	19,742,267	0

Clinton had won a convincing 43 percent of the popular vote, compared to 38 percent for Bush, and 19 percent for Perot.

As they learned the news of their victory, Clinton's supporters rejoiced in the streets of Little Rock, Arkansas. They shouted, cheered, hugged, and waved victory

Supreme Court Justice William Rehnquist (right) delivers the oath of office to the new president.

banners. Appearing on an outdoor platform at the statehouse, Clinton joyfully thanked them: "My fellow Americans, with high hopes and brave hearts, in massive numbers, the American people have voted to make a new beginning."

President Bill Clinton's inauguration came on January 20, 1993. Standing beside Hillary in the crisp, wintry air outside the Capitol, with one hand on the Bible, and the other raised, Clinton recited the presidential oath: "I, William Jefferson Clinton, do solemnly swear that I will faithfully execute the office of president of the United States, and will to the best of my ability, preserve, protect, and defend the Constitution of the United States."

In June 1993, President Clinton appointed Kristine
Gebbie to be the nation's first AIDS policy coordinator.

Chapter 8

Learning How Washington Works

Eighteen people joined President Clinton's administration as heads of government departments, replacing those from the Bush administration. Past presidents had filled most of these posts with white men. During his campaign, Clinton had promised to make his cabinet "look more like America." As a result, his cabinet included five women, four African Americans, and two Latinos.

Although most of his appointments were easily approved by the Senate, Clinton ran into immediate trouble when he nominated Zoë Baird as attorney general. Although Baird was a highly respected lawyer, a routine investigation showed she had broken laws she would be called upon to enforce as attorney general. She had knowingly employed two illegal aliens from Peru in her home and had failed to pay taxes on their wages. On January 14, under intense pressure, Clinton withdrew her nomination.

Clinton eventually chose Janet Reno for attorney general, and she was easily approved by the Senate. As the attorney general for the state of Florida, she had fought a rising tide of violence and drugs. Perceived as tough and honest, Reno became the nation's first woman attorney general.

More controversy daunted Clinton's early administration when he attempted to fulfill a campaign promise to lift the long-standing ban on homosexuals in the U.S. military. Clinton signed an executive order forcing recruiting officers to stop asking recruits about their sexual preference. He also ordered that any disciplinary actions should be dropped against homosexuals who had not committed "offenses of conduct."

Clinton's order angered many high-ranking officers. They believed the presence of openly gay people in the military caused too many problems and weakened morale. In the end, Clinton had to compromise. A policy of "don't ask, don't tell," was agreed upon. Recruiters would no longer ask recruits whether they were homosexual, but open homosexuality still would not be tolerated.

Another big error in judgment came when Clinton made the mistake of getting a $200 haircut that cost tax-payers $5,300 while his plane waited on the runway for the stylist to finish.

Clinton also aroused criticism when he attended a Memorial Day ceremony at the national Vietnam Veterans Memorial. Some veterans' groups were displeased that Clinton, who had avoided the draft, would appear at this memorial. The black granite wall lists the names of all those killed in the war. Clinton knelt to make a rubbing of

President Clinton is filled with grim emotion as he ponders the Vietnam
Veterans Memorial.

the name of one of his childhood friends. He made a
speech, during which some people jeered, calling him a
"draft dodger."

Most people, however, were glad that Clinton had
appeared at the memorial. They thought it was a brave and
strong gesture to ignore those who did not want him there.
As commander in chief, Clinton felt it was part of his duty
to attend the military ceremony and show he cared about
the sacrifices made by soldiers in Vietnam.

To many people, Clinton's early months in the White House appeared disorganized and were marred by too many errors of judgment. But as his first year wore on, Clinton began to enjoy some victories. In February 1993, he signed the Family Leave Bill. This new law required companies to allow workers who had new babies or family troubles to take up to twelve weeks of unpaid leave without losing their jobs. The same bill had been passed twice by Congress only to be vetoed by President Bush. Clinton said, "The first bill I'm to sign as president truly puts people first. I am very appreciative that the Congress has moved so rapidly."

Clinton also won approval when he filled a vacated spot on the Supreme Court with Ruth Bader Ginsburg. Ginsburg, a judge on the Federal Appeals court and a pioneering feminist lawyer, became the second woman to sit on the Court.

But President Clinton's hardest work came when he rolled up his sleeves and dealt with the struggling national economy. Many had been angered that the new president spent so much time and energy on an issue like the military ban on homosexuals. This was an issue that affected relatively few people. The troubled economy was on everyone's mind, and people had expected him to address that issue first.

So on February 16, Clinton addressed members of the House and Senate. He announced several bold changes he wanted to make to address the country's troubles. "Our

President Clinton addresses Congress in February 1993 in his first State of the Union address.

nation needs a new direction," he said. "Tonight, I present to you a comprehensive plan to set our nation on that new course."

Clinton vowed to create new jobs for the unemployed; improve the school system; fix the slumping economy; and submit a national budget that would reduce the deficit. And he announced that the most important task he would undertake was to revise the national health-care system.

Hillary Rodham Clinton conducts a meeting about health-care reform with more than 100 doctors.

For years, the rising cost of health care had grown out of control. The United States was spending far more than any other country on medical care—$800 billion a year! More and more Americans were unable to afford the high cost of health insurance and were left unprotected when someone in their family became ill.

President Clinton announced that Hillary Rodham Clinton would head a special task force that would study the problem and write a new health care plan for the United States. If he could revise the health-care system, Clinton knew, this would be the biggest achievement of his administration.

Heading this task force was by far the most complex and important position ever held by a First Lady. Clinton said he did not hire Hillary because she was his wife, but because she was the most capable person he knew for the job.

President Clinton and Vice President Gore hard at work

While his wife went to work on health care, President Clinton went to work on the national budget. The plan he and his staff soon came up with would cut sharply into the deficit. But to save money, he would have to raise taxes and cut spending in hundreds of important programs.

The Clinton budget drew immediate attacks from Republicans. They claimed the government should cut more programs and not raise taxes so much. Clinton talked tough, declaring, "Show me where [to cut] and be specific—not hot air!"

Clinton knew he would have to rally public support for his budget to pass in Congress. So he did what proved to work during his campaign—he went to the people. Clinton, Al Gore, and several cabinet members fanned out across the country to campaign for the new plan. Clinton said, "My fellow Americans, the test of this plan cannot be 'what is in it for me?' It has got to be 'what is in it for us?'"

The budget battle was long and hard. Clinton campaigned day and night, telephoning members of Congress for months. In the end, Clinton decided to compromise on many points in his bill so that he could get the entire bill passed. The Clinton budget did pass Congress, but the new president had learned hard lessons about the give and take of federal law making.

During the budget struggle, Clinton had many other issues to worry about. A terrible civil war was raging in Bosnia-Hercegovina, part of the former European nation of Yugoslavia. Some people wanted the United States to take military action to stop the fighting. Others argued such a step would be disastrous. As a compromise, Clinton decided to begin an airlift of food and medical supplies to those affected by the fighting.

In Russia's new leader, Boris Yeltsin, Clinton found someone also struggling to change his country in profound ways. Yeltsin was trying to bring democracy to a region long dominated by communism. At the end of March 1993, Clinton and Yeltsin met in Vancouver, British Columbia, to discuss how the United States could help support Yeltsin's initiatives. Clinton pledged millions of dollars in economic assistance to Russia. The long Cold War with Russia was over, Clinton explained, and it was time to start "investing in peace."

On June 26, 1993, Clinton made perhaps his toughest decision as president. It had been revealed that Iraqi president Saddam Hussein had engineered an assassination attempt on ex-president George Bush, who had been traveling in Kuwait. The attempt had failed, but President Clinton knew he had to strike back, quickly and decisively. After giving the matter much thought, he ordered Tomahawk cruise missiles to be launched against the Iraqi intelligence agency, a huge building in the center of Baghdad. Clinton then went on television to explain his actions to the nation: "From the first days of our Revolution, American security has depended on the clarity of this message: Don't tread on us."

Clinton also showed himself to be a strong leader at the "G-7" Summit in Tokyo, Japan. The G-7 are the seven most powerful industrialized countries—The United States, Great Britain, Canada, Germany, France, Italy, and Japan. This was Clinton's first test as a world leader, and he successfully convinced the G-7 to agree on a $3 billion aid package for Yeltsin and Russia's struggling democracy.

President Clinton made his mark in world politics when he met with Russian president Boris Yeltsin.

Chapter 9

The President Is Victorious

Bill Clinton's greatest first-year achievements were yet to come. The new president had been just a governor with no experience in foreign affairs, yet he engineered an historic summit between longtime enemies Israel and the Palestine Liberation Organization. In September 1993, Israel's prime minister Yitzhak Rabin and PLO leader Yassir Arafat met face to face for the first time in years during a ceremony on the south lawn of the White House. They signed a peace agreement, and then President Clinton pulled the two men together, prompting them to shake hands and confirm their agreement. In the coming months, the continuing Middle East peace talks ran into trouble. But the world agreed that when Bill Clinton coaxed Rabin and Arafat to shake hands, it had been a monumental step forward.

Throughout his first year in office, Clinton astounded everyone with his energy, enthusiasm, and willingness to tackle difficult tasks. Passage of the North American Free Trade Agreement (NAFTA) required a tremendous effort on Clinton's part. The idea behind NAFTA was simple. The agreement would remove virtually all trade

Top: President Clinton's most stunning victory came with the historic handshake of Rabin (left) and Arafat (right) at the White House.
Bottom: All of Clinton's achievements are the result countless hours of hard work in the Oval Office.

restrictions between Canada, the United States, and Mexico. Those who supported the plan believed it would create vast new markets for American products, thus creating new jobs and business opportunities across the country. Opponents argued that American factories would leave the United States and go to Mexico. There, workers were paid far less than the wages demanded by Americans.

In his fight for passage of NAFTA, Clinton showed he could stay up late, get up early, and keep an impossible schedule going for days on end.

Clinton was backed by all five of the living former presidents as well as many economists. In the end, however, it came down to making hundreds of phone calls to convince members of Congress. In the last days before the vote, Clinton had to "cut a lot of deals" but he got the votes needed. Many saw his unshakable effort to win approval for NAFTA as proof that Clinton had the leadership it took to be a great president. It gave him renewed confidence.

Speaker of the House Tom Foley said after the vote, "Mr. Clinton worked harder than any president I've seen, on any issue. And I've been here thirty years!" Clinton, happy and exhausted, his voice hoarse, said, "At a time when many of our people are hurting from the strains of this tough global economy, we choose to compete, not retreat."

Bill Clinton survived many painful battles in his first year in office. But more painful than any attack on his

President Clinton marked a full year in office with his January 1994 State of the Union address.

character or ideas was the loss of his mother. On January 7, 1994, Virginia Clinton Kelly died in her sleep. She was seventy years old. Though she'd battled breast cancer for several years, her death was sudden and shocked the president. Deeply saddened, he hurried back to Arkansas for her funeral.

Virginia Clinton Kelly, a nurse for more than thirty years, had suffered much hardship in her life—family drug and alcohol addiction, divorce, an abusive husband, and then cancer. Throughout it all, she remained a loving, strong-willed, and optimistic person. Bill Clinton had learned a great deal about strength in the face of pain from her example.

On January 23, 1994, standing before members of the House, Senate, judicial branches of government, and a huge television audience, President Clinton delivered the State of the Union address.

Most Americans were concerned about a sharp rise in violent crime. In many of the nation's cities, armed gangs turned some neighborhoods into virtual war zones. Clinton discussed his new crime bill which, he hoped, would "give our young people the chance to walk to school in safety and to be in school in safety instead of dodging bullets." The bill called for funding to put more police officers on the streets, stricter gun laws, and a "three strikes and you're out" rule—life sentences for three-time violent offenders.

President Clinton again discussed the health-care crisis

and the continuing danger of rising national debt. He outlined his plans to reform the welfare system and the need for America to remain competetive in a global economy by retraining workers and improving efficiency.

But the most compelling moments in his speech came when he asked Americans to "pull together" and care for each other: "Let's be honest. Our problems go way beyond the scope of government. They're rooted in the loss of values and the disappearance of work and the breakdown of our families and our communities. My fellow Americans, we can cut the deficit, create jobs, promote democracy around the world, pass welfare reform and health care, and pass the toughest crime bill in history, and still leave too many of our people behind. . . . The American people have got to want to change from within if we're going to bring back work and family and community."

Clinton went on to praise those who helped neighbors and strangers during the 1993 summer floods in the Midwest and the fires that had recently ravaged parts of California. He urged that the same spirit of community be within us all the time. "Let us not reserve the better angels only for natural disasters, leaving our deepest and most profound problems to petty political fighting. Let us instead be true to our spirit, facing facts, coming together, and bringing hope and moving forward."

President Bill Clinton had weathered a difficult first year in office. He had overcome early mistakes. Now he looked ahead with hope toward the challenges of his next three years as U.S. president.

Chronology of American History

(Shaded area covers events in William Clinton's lifetime.)

About A.D. 982 — Eric the Red, born in Norway, reaches Greenland in one of the first European voyages to North America.

About 1000 — Leif Ericson (Eric the Red's son) leads what is thought to be the first European expedition to mainland North America; Leif probably lands in Canada.

1492 — Christopher Columbus, seeking a sea route from Spain to the Far East, discovers the New World.

1497 — John Cabot reaches Canada in the first English voyage to North America.

1513 — Ponce de León explores Florida in search of the fabled Fountain of Youth.

1519-1521 — Hernando Cortés of Spain conquers Mexico.

1534 — French explorers led by Jacques Cartier enter the Gulf of St. Lawrence in Canada.

1540 — Spanish explorer Francisco Coronado begins exploring the American Southwest, seeking the riches of the mythical Seven Cities of Cibola.

1565 — St. Augustine, Florida, the first permanent European town in what is now the United States, is founded by the Spanish.

1607 — Jamestown, Virginia, is founded, the first permanent English town in the present-day U.S.

1608 — Frenchman Samuel de Champlain founds the village of Quebec, Canada.

1609 — Henry Hudson explores the eastern coast of present-day U.S. for the Netherlands; the Dutch then claim parts of New York, New Jersey, Delaware, and Connecticut and name the area New Netherland.

1619 — The English colonies' first shipment of black slaves arrives in Jamestown.

1620 — English Pilgrims found Massachusetts' first permanent town at Plymouth.

1621 — Massachusetts Pilgrims and Indians hold the famous first Thanksgiving feast in colonial America.

1623 — Colonization of New Hampshire is begun by the English.

1624 — Colonization of present-day New York State is begun by the Dutch at Fort Orange (Albany).

1625 — The Dutch start building New Amsterdam (now New York City).

1630 — The town of Boston, Massachusetts, is founded by the English Puritans.

1633 — Colonization of Connecticut is begun by the English.

1634 — Colonization of Maryland is begun by the English.

1636 — Harvard, the colonies' first college, is founded in Massachusetts. Rhode Island colonization begins when Englishman Roger Williams founds Providence.

1638 — Delaware colonization begins as Swedes build Fort Christina at present-day Wilmington.

1640 — Stephen Daye of Cambridge, Massachusetts, prints *The Bay Psalm Book*, the first English-language book published in what is now the U.S.

1643 — Swedish settlers begin colonizing Pennsylvania.

About 1650 — North Carolina is colonized by Virginia settlers.

1660 — New Jersey colonization is begun by the Dutch at present-day Jersey City.

1670 — South Carolina colonization is begun by the English near Charleston.

1673 — Jacques Marquette and Louis Jolliet explore the upper Mississippi River for France.

1682 — Philadelphia, Pennsylvania, is settled. La Salle explores Mississippi River all the way to its mouth in Louisiana and claims the whole Mississippi Valley for France.

1693 — College of William and Mary is founded in Williamsburg, Virginia.

1700 — Colonial population is about 250,000.

1703—Benjamin Franklin is born in Boston,

1732—George Washington, first president of the U.S., is born in Westmoreland County, Virginia.

1733—James Oglethorpe founds Savannah, Georgia; Georgia is established as the thirteenth colony.

1735—John Adams, second president of the U.S., is born in Braintree, Massachusetts.

1737—William Byrd founds Richmond, Virginia.

1738—British troops are sent to Georgia over border dispute with Spain.

1739—Black insurrection takes place in South Carolina.

1740—English Parliament passes act allowing naturalization of immigrants to American colonies after seven-year residence.

1743—Thomas Jefferson is born in Albemarle County, Virginia. Benjamin Franklin retires at age thirty-seven to devote himself to scientific inquiries and public service.

1744—King George's War begins; France joins war effort against England.

1745—During King George's War, France raids settlements in Maine and New York.

1747—Classes begin at Princeton College in New Jersey.

1748—The Treaty of Aix-la-Chapelle concludes King George's War.

1749—Parliament legally recognizes slavery in colonies and the inauguration of the plantation system in the South. George Washington becomes the surveyor for Culpepper County in Virginia.

1750—Thomas Walker passes through and names Cumberland Gap on his way toward Kentucky region. Colonial population is about 1,200,000.

1751—James Madison, fourth president of the U.S., is born in Port Conway, Virginia. English Parliament passes Currency Act, banning New England colonies from issuing paper money. George Washington travels to Barbados.

1752—Pennsylvania Hospital, the first general hospital in the colonies, is founded in Philadelphia. Benjamin Franklin uses a kite in a thunderstorm to demonstrate that lightning is a form of electricity.

1753—George Washington delivers command that the French withdraw from the Ohio River Valley; French disregard the demand. Colonial population is about 1,328,000.

1754—French and Indian War begins (extends to Europe as the Seven Years' War). Washington surrenders at Fort Necessity.

1755—French and Indians ambush Braddock. Washington becomes commander of Virginia troops.

1756—England declares war on France.

1758—James Monroe, fifth president of the U.S., is born in Westmoreland County, Virginia.

1759—Cherokee Indian war begins in southern colonies; hostilities extend to 1761. George Washington marries Martha Dandridge Custis.

1760—George III becomes king of England. Colonial population is about 1,600,000.

1762—England declares war on Spain.

1763—Treaty of Paris concludes the French and Indian War and the Seven Years' War. England gains Canada and most other French lands east of the Mississippi River.

1764—British pass the Sugar Act to gain tax money from the colonists. The issue of taxation without representation is first introduced in Boston. John Adams marries Abigail Smith.

1765—Stamp Act goes into effect in the colonies. Business virtually stops as almost all colonists refuse to use the stamps.

1766—British repeal the Stamp Act.

1767—John Quincy Adams, sixth president of the U.S. and son of second president John Adams, is born in Braintree, Massachusetts. Andrew Jackson, seventh president of the U.S., is born in Waxhaw settlement, South Carolina.

1769—Daniel Boone sights the Kentucky Territory.

1770—In the Boston Massacre, British soldiers kill five colonists and injure six. Townshend Acts are repealed, thus eliminating all duties on imports to the colonies except the tax on tea.

1771—Benjamin Franklin begins his autobiography, a work that he will never complete. The North Carolina assembly passes the "Bloody Act," which makes rioters guilty of treason.

1772—Samuel Adams rouses colonists to consider British threats to self-government.

1773—English Parliament passes the Tea Act. Colonists dressed as Mohawk Indians board British tea ships and toss 342 casks of tea into the water in what becomes known as the Boston Tea Party. William Henry Harrison is born in Charles City County, Virginia.

1774—British close the port of Boston to punish the city for the Boston Tea Party. First Continental Congress convenes in Philadelphia.

1775—American Revolution begins with battles of Lexington and Concord, Massachusetts. Second Continental Congress opens in Philadelphia. George Washington becomes commander-in-chief of the Continental army.

1776—Declaration of Independence is adopted on July 4.

1777—Congress adopts the American flag with thirteen stars and thirteen stripes. John Adams is sent to France to negotiate peace treaty.

1778—France declares war against Great Britain and becomes U.S. ally.

1779—British surrender to Americans at Vincennes. Thomas Jefferson is elected governor of Virginia. James Madison is elected to the Continental Congress.

1780—Benedict Arnold, first American traitor, defects to the British.

1781—Articles of Confederation go into effect. Cornwallis surrenders to George Washington at Yorktown, ending the American Revolution.

1782—American commissioners, including John Adams, sign peace treaty with British in Paris. Thomas Jefferson's wife, Martha, dies. Martin Van Buren is born in Kinderhook, New York.

1784—Zachary Taylor is born near Barboursville, Virginia.

1785—Congress adopts the dollar as the unit of currency. John Adams is made minister to Great Britain. Thomas Jefferson is appointed minister to France.

1786—Shays' Rebellion begins in Massachusetts.

1787—Constitutional Convention assembles in Philadelphia, with George Washington presiding; U.S. Constitution is adopted. Delaware, New Jersey, and Pennsylvania become states.

1788—Virginia, South Carolina, New York, Connecticut, New Hampshire, Maryland, and Massachusetts become states. U.S. Constitution is ratified. New York City is declared U.S. capital.

1789—Presidential electors elect George Washington and John Adams as first president and vice-president. Thomas Jefferson is appointed secretary of state. North Carolina becomes a state. French Revolution begins.

1790—Supreme Court meets for the first time. Rhode Island becomes a state. First national census in the U.S. counts 3,929,214 persons. John Tyler is born in Charles City County, Virginia.

1791—Vermont enters the Union. U.S. Bill of Rights, the first ten amendments to the Constitution, goes into effect. District of Columbia is established. James Buchanan is born in Stony Batter, Pennsylvania.

1792—Thomas Paine publishes *The Rights of Man*. Kentucky becomes a state. Two political parties are formed in the U.S., Federalist and Republican. Washington is elected to a second term, with Adams as vice-president.

1793—War between France and Britain begins; U.S. declares neutrality. Eli Whitney invents the cotton gin; cotton production and slave labor increase in the South.

1794—Eleventh Amendment to the Constitution is passed, limiting federal courts' power. "Whiskey Rebellion" in Pennsylvania protests federal whiskey tax. James Madison marries Dolley Payne Todd.

1795—George Washington signs the Jay Treaty with Great Britain. Treaty of San Lorenzo, between U.S. and Spain, settles Florida boundary and gives U.S. right to navigate the Mississippi. James Polk is born near Pineville, North Carolina.

1796—Tennessee enters the Union. Washington gives his Farewell Address, refusing a third presidential term. John Adams is elected president and Thomas Jefferson vice-president.

1797—Adams recommends defense measures against possible war with France. Napoleon Bonaparte and his army march against Austrians in Italy. U.S. population is about 4,900,000.

1798—Washington is named commander-in-chief of the U.S. Army. Department of the Navy is created. Alien and Sedition Acts are passed. Napoleon's troops invade Egypt and Switzerland.

1799—George Washington dies at Mount Vernon, New York. James Monroe is elected governor of Virginia. French Revolution ends. Napoleon becomes ruler of France.

1800—Thomas Jefferson and Aaron Burr tie for president. U.S. capital is moved from Philadelphia to Washington, D.C. The White House is built as presidents' home. Spain returns Louisiana to France. Millard Fillmore is born in Locke, New York.

1801—After thirty-six ballots, House of Representatives elects Thomas Jefferson president, making Burr vice-president. James Madison is named secretary of state.

1802—Congress abolishes excise taxes. U.S. Military Academy is founded at West Point, New York.

1803—Ohio enters the Union. Louisiana Purchase treaty is signed with France, greatly expanding U.S. territory.

1804—Twelfth Amendment to the Constitution rules that president and vice-president be elected separately. Alexander Hamilton is killed by Vice-President Aaron Burr in a duel. Orleans Territory is established. Napoleon crowns himself emperor of France. Franklin Pierce is born in Hillsborough Lower Village, New Hampshire.

1805—Thomas Jefferson begins his second term as president. Lewis and Clark expedition reaches the Pacific Ocean.

1806—Coinage of silver dollars is stopped; resumes in 1836.

1807—Aaron Burr is acquitted in treason trial. Embargo Act closes U.S. ports to trade.

1808—James Madison is elected president. Congress outlaws importing slaves from Africa. Andrew Johnson is born in Raleigh, North Carolina.

1809—Abraham Lincoln is born near Hodgenville, Kentucky.

1810—U.S. population is 7,240,000.

1811—William Henry Harrison defeats Indians at Tippecanoe. Monroe is named secretary of state.

1812—Louisiana becomes a state. U.S. declares war on Britain (War of 1812). James Madison is reelected president. Napoleon invades Russia.

1813—British forces take Fort Niagara and Buffalo, New York.

1814—Francis Scott Key writes "The Star-Spangled Banner." British troops burn much of Washington, D.C., including the White House. Treaty of Ghent ends War of 1812. James Monroe becomes secretary of war.

1815—Napoleon meets his final defeat at Battle of Waterloo.

1816—James Monroe is elected president. Indiana becomes a state.

1817—Mississippi becomes a state. Construction on Erie Canal begins.

1818—Illinois enters the Union. The present thirteen-stripe flag is adopted. Border between U.S. and Canada is agreed upon.

1819—Alabama becomes a state. U.S. purchases Florida from Spain. Thomas Jefferson establishes the University of Virginia.

1820—James Monroe is reelected. In the Missouri Compromise, Maine enters the Union as a free (non-slave) state.

1821—Missouri enters the Union as a slave state. Santa Fe Trail opens the American Southwest. Mexico declares independence from Spain. Napoleon Bonaparte dies.

1822—U.S. recognizes Mexico and Colombia. Liberia in Africa is founded as a home for freed slaves. Ulysses S. Grant is born in Point Pleasant, Ohio. Rutherford B. Hayes is born in Delaware, Ohio.

1823—Monroe Doctrine closes North and South America to European colonizing or invasion.

1824—House of Representatives elects John Quincy Adams president when none of the four candidates wins a majority in national election. Mexico becomes a republic.

1825—Erie Canal is opened. U.S. population is 11,300,000.

1826—Thomas Jefferson and John Adams both die on July 4, the fiftieth anniversary of the Declaration of Independence.

1828—Andrew Jackson is elected president. Tariff of Abominations is passed, cutting imports.

1829—James Madison attends Virginia's constitutional convention. Slavery is abolished in Mexico. Chester A. Arthur is born in Fairfield, Vermont.

1830—Indian Removal Act to resettle Indians west of the Mississippi is approved.

1831—James Monroe dies in New York City. James A. Garfield is born in Orange, Ohio. Cyrus McCormick develops his reaper.

1832—Andrew Jackson, nominated by the new Democratic Party, is reelected president.

1833—Britain abolishes slavery in its colonies. Benjamin Harrison is born in North Bend, Ohio.

1835—Federal government becomes debt-free for the first time.

1836—Martin Van Buren becomes president. Texas wins independence from Mexico. Arkansas joins the Union. James Madison dies at Montpelier, Virginia.

1837—Michigan enters the Union. U.S. population is 15,900,000. Grover Cleveland is born in Caldwell, New Jersey.

1840—William Henry Harrison is elected president.

1841—President Harrison dies in Washington, D.C., one month after inauguration. Vice-President John Tyler succeeds him.

1843—William McKinley is born in Niles, Ohio.

1844—James Knox Polk is elected president. Samuel Morse sends first telegraphic message.

1845—Texas and Florida become states. Potato famine in Ireland causes massive emigration from Ireland to U.S. Andrew Jackson dies near Nashville, Tennessee.

1846—Iowa enters the Union. War with Mexico begins.

1847—U.S. captures Mexico City.

1848—John Quincy Adams dies in Washington, D.C. Zachary Taylor becomes president. Treaty of Guadalupe Hidalgo ends Mexico-U.S. war. Wisconsin becomes a state.

1849—James Polk dies in Nashville, Tennessee.

1850—President Taylor dies in Washington, D.C.; Vice-President Millard Fillmore succeeds him. California enters the Union, breaking tie between slave and free states.

1852—Franklin Pierce is elected president.

1853—Gadsden Purchase transfers Mexican territory to U.S.

1854—"War for Bleeding Kansas" is fought between slave and free states.

1855—Czar Nicholas I of Russia dies, succeeded by Alexander II.

1856—James Buchanan is elected president. In Massacre of Potawatomi Creek, Kansas-slavers are murdered by free-staters. Woodrow Wilson is born in Staunton, Virginia.

1857—William Howard Taft is born in Cincinnati, Ohio.

1858—Minnesota enters the Union. Theodore Roosevelt is born in New York City.

1859—Oregon becomes a state.

1860—Abraham Lincoln is elected president; South Carolina secedes from the Union in protest.

1861—Arkansas, Tennessee, North Carolina, and Virginia secede. Kansas enters the Union as a free state. Civil War begins.

1862—Union forces capture Fort Henry, Roanoke Island, Fort Donelson, Jacksonville, and New Orleans; Union armies are defeated at the battles of Bull Run and Fredericksburg. Martin Van Buren dies in Kinderhook, New York. John Tyler dies near Charles City, Virginia.

1863—Lincoln issues Emancipation Proclamation: all slaves held in rebelling territories are declared free. West Virginia becomes a state.

1864—Abraham Lincoln is reelected. Nevada becomes a state.

1865 — Lincoln is assassinated in Washington, D.C., and succeeded by Andrew Johnson. U.S. Civil War ends on May 26. Thirteenth Amendment abolishes slavery. Warren G. Harding is born in Blooming Grove, Ohio.

1867 — Nebraska becomes a state. U.S. buys Alaska from Russia for $7,200,000. Reconstruction Acts are passed.

1868 — President Johnson is impeached for violating Tenure of Office Act, but is acquitted by Senate. Ulysses S. Grant is elected president. Fourteenth Amendment prohibits voting discrimination. James Buchanan dies in Lancaster, Pennsylvania.

1869 — Franklin Pierce dies in Concord, New Hampshire.

1870 — Fifteenth Amendment gives blacks the right to vote.

1872 — Grant is reelected over Horace Greeley. General Amnesty Act pardons ex-Confederates. Calvin Coolidge is born in Plymouth Notch, Vermont.

1874 — Millard Fillmore dies in Buffalo, New York. Herbert Hoover is born in West Branch, Iowa.

1875 — Andrew Johnson dies in Carter's Station, Tennessee.

1876 — Colorado enters the union. Battle of the Little Big Horn is fought in Montana: George Armstrong Custer and 200 troopers of the Seventh Cavalry are killed by Native Americans.

1877 — Rutherford B. Hayes is elected president as all disputed votes are awarded to him.

1880 — James A. Garfield is elected president.

1881 — President Garfield is assassinated and dies in Elberon, New Jersey. Vice-President Chester A. Arthur succeeds him.

1882 — U.S. bans Chinese immigration. Franklin D. Roosevelt is born in Hyde Park, New York.

1884 — Grover Cleveland is elected president.

1885 — Ulysses S. Grant dies in Mount McGregor, New York.

1886 — Statue of Liberty is dedicated. Chester A. Arthur dies in New York City.

1888 — Benjamin Harrison is elected president.

1889 — North Dakota, South Dakota, Washington, and Montana become states.

1890 — Dwight D. Eisenhower is born in Denison, Texas. Idaho and Wyoming become states.

1892 — Grover Cleveland is elected president.

1893 — Rutherford B. Hayes dies in Fremont, Ohio.

1896 — William McKinley is elected president. Utah becomes a state.

1898 — U.S. declares war on Spain over Cuba.

1900 — McKinley is reelected. Boxer Rebellion against foreigners in China begins.

1901 — McKinley is assassinated by anarchist Leon Czolgosz in Buffalo, New York; Theodore Roosevelt becomes president. Benjamin Harrison dies in Indianapolis, Indiana.

1902 — U.S. acquires perpetual control over Panama Canal.

1903 — Alaskan frontier is settled.

1904 — Russian-Japanese War breaks out. Theodore Roosevelt wins presidential election.

1905 — Treaty of Portsmouth signed, ending Russian-Japanese War.

1906 — U.S. troops occupy Cuba.

1907 — President Roosevelt bars all Japanese immigration. Oklahoma enters the Union.

1908 — William Howard Taft becomes president. Grover Cleveland dies in Princeton, New Jersey. Lyndon B. Johnson is born near Stonewall, Texas.

1909 — NAACP is founded under W.E.B. DuBois

1910 — China abolishes slavery.

1911 — Chinese Revolution begins. Ronald Reagan is born in Tampico, Illinois.

1912 — Woodrow Wilson is elected president. Arizona and New Mexico become states.

1913—Federal income tax is introduced in U.S. through the Sixteenth Amendment. Richard Nixon is born in Yorba Linda, California. Gerald Ford is born in Omaha, Nebraska.

1914—World War I begins.

1915—British liner *Lusitania* is sunk by German submarine.

1916—Wilson is reelected president.

1917—U.S. breaks diplomatic relations with Germany. Czar Nicholas II of Russia abdicates as revolution begins. U.S. declares war on Austria-Hungary. John F. Kennedy is born in Brookline, Massachusetts.

1918—Wilson proclaims "Fourteen Points" as war aims. On November 11, armistice is signed between Allies and Germany.

1919—Eighteenth Amendment prohibits sale and manufacture of intoxicating liquors. Wilson presides over first League of Nations; wins Nobel Peace Prize. Theodore Roosevelt dies in Oyster Bay, New York.

1920—Nineteenth Amendment (women's suffrage) is passed. Warren Harding is elected president.

1921—Adolf Hitler's storm troopers begin to terrorize political opponents.

1922—Irish Free State is established. Soviet states form USSR. Benito Mussolini forms Fascist government in Italy.

1923—President Harding dies in San Francisco, California; he is succeeded by Vice-President Calvin Coolidge.

1924—Coolidge is elected president. Woodrow Wilson dies in Washington, D.C. James Carter is born in Plains, Georgia. George Bush is born in Milton, Massachusetts.

1925—Hitler reorganizes Nazi Party and publishes first volume of *Mein Kampf.*

1926—Fascist youth organizations founded in Germany and Italy. Republic of Lebanon proclaimed.

1927—Stalin becomes Soviet dictator. Economic conference in Geneva attended by fifty-two nations.

1928—Herbert Hoover is elected president. U.S. and many other nations sign Kellogg-Briand pacts to outlaw war.

1929—Stock prices in New York crash on "Black Thursday"; the Great Depression begins.

1930—Bank of U.S. and its many branches close (most significant bank failure of the year). William Howard Taft dies in Washington, D.C.

1931—Emigration from U.S. exceeds immigration for first time as Depression deepens.

1932—Franklin D. Roosevelt wins presidential election in a Democratic landslide.

1933—First concentration camps are erected in Germany. U.S. recognizes USSR and resumes trade. Twenty-First Amendment repeals prohibition. Calvin Coolidge dies in Northampton, Massachusetts.

1934—Severe dust storms hit Plains states. President Roosevelt passes U.S. Social Security Act.

1936—Roosevelt is reelected. Spanish Civil War begins. Hitler and Mussolini form Rome-Berlin Axis.

1937—Roosevelt signs Neutrality Act.

1938—Roosevelt sends appeal to Hitler and Mussolini to settle European problems amicably.

1939—Germany takes over Czechoslovakia and invades Poland, starting World War II.

1940—Roosevelt is reelected for a third term.

1941—Japan bombs Pearl Harbor. U.S. declares war on Japan. Germany and Italy declare war on U.S.; U.S. then declares war on them.

1942—Allies agree not to make separate peace treaties with the enemies. U.S. government transfers more than 100,000 Nisei (Japanese-Americans) from west coast to inland concentration camps.

1943—Allied bombings of Germany begin.

1944—Roosevelt is reelected for a fourth term. Allied forces invade Normandy on D-Day.

1945—President Franklin D. Roosevelt dies in Warm Springs, Georgia; Vice-President Harry S. Truman succeeds him. Mussolini is killed; Hitler commits suicide. Germany surrenders. U.S. drops atomic bomb on Hiroshima; Japan surrenders: World War II ends.

1946—U.N. General Assembly holds its first session in London. Peace conference of twenty-one nations is held in Paris. William Jefferson Clinton is born in Hope, Arkansas.

1947—Peace treaties are signed in Paris. "Cold War" is in full swing.

1948—U.S. passes Marshall Plan Act, providing $17 billion in aid for Europe. U.S. recognizes new nation of Israel. India and Pakistan become free of British rule. Truman is elected president.

1949—Republic of Eire is proclaimed in Dublin. Russia blocks land route access from Western Germany to Berlin; airlift begins. U.S., France, and Britain agree to merge their zones of occupation in West Germany. Apartheid program begins in South Africa.

1950—Riots occur in Johannesburg, South Africa, against apartheid. North Korea invades South Korea. U.N. forces land in South Korea and recapture Seoul.

1951—Twenty-Second Amendment limits president to two terms.

1952—Dwight D. Eisenhower resigns as supreme commander in Europe and is elected president.

1953—Stalin dies; struggle for power in Russia follows. Rosenbergs are executed for espionage.

1954—U.S. and Japan sign mutual defense agreement.

1955—Blacks in Montgomery, Alabama, boycott segregated bus lines.

1956—Eisenhower is reelected president. Soviet troops march into Hungary.

1957—U.S. agrees to withdraw ground forces from Japan. Russia launches first satellite, *Sputnik.*

1958—European Common Market comes into being. Fidel Castro begins war against Batista government in Cuba.

1959—Alaska becomes the forty-ninth state. Hawaii becomes fiftieth state. Castro becomes premier of Cuba. De Gaulle is proclaimed president of the Fifth Republic of France.

1960—Historic debates between Senator John F. Kennedy and Vice-President Richard Nixon are televised. Kennedy is elected president. Brezhnev becomes president of USSR.

1961—Berlin Wall is constructed. Kennedy and Khrushchev confer in Vienna. In Bay of Pigs incident, Cubans trained by CIA attempt to overthrow Castro.

1962—U.S. military council is established in South Vietnam.

1963—Riots and beatings by police and whites mark civil rights demonstrations in Birmingham, Alabama; 30,000 troops are called out. Martin Luther King, Jr., is arrested. Freedom marchers descend on Washington, D.C., to demonstrate. President Kennedy is assassinated in Dallas, Texas; Vice-President Lyndon B. Johnson is sworn in as president.

1964—U.S. aircraft bomb North Vietnam. Johnson is elected president. Herbert Hoover dies in New York City.

1965—U.S. combat troops arrive in South Vietnam.

1966—Thousands protest U.S. policy in Vietnam. National Guard quells race riots in Chicago.

1967—Six-Day War occurs between Israel and Arab nations.

1968—Martin Luther King, Jr., is assassinated in Memphis, Tennessee. Senator Robert Kennedy is assassinated in Los Angeles. Riots and police brutality take place at Democratic National Convention in Chicago. Richard Nixon is elected president. Czechoslovakia is invaded by Soviet troops.

1969—Dwight D. Eisenhower dies in Washington, D.C. Hundreds of thousands of people in several U.S. cities demonstrate against Vietnam War.

1970—Four Vietnam War protesters are killed by National Guardsmen at Kent State University in Ohio.

1971—Twenty-Sixth Amendment allows eighteen-year-olds to vote.

1972—Nixon visits Communist China; is reelected president in near-record landslide. Watergate affair begins when five men are arrested in the Watergate hotel complex in Washington, D.C. Nixon announces resignations of aides Haldeman, Ehrlichman, and Dean and Attorney General Kleindienst as a result of Watergate-related charges. Harry S. Truman dies in Kansas City, Missouri.

1973—Vice-President Spiro Agnew resigns; Gerald Ford is named vice-president. Vietnam peace treaty is formally approved after nineteen months of negotiations. Lyndon B. Johnson dies in San Antonio, Texas.

1974—As a result of Watergate cover-up, impeachment is considered; Nixon resigns and Ford becomes president. Ford pardons Nixon and grants limited amnesty to Vietnam War draft evaders and military deserters.

1975—U.S. civilians are evacuated from Saigon, South Vietnam, as Communist forces complete takeover of South Vietnam.

1976—U.S. celebrates its Bicentennial. James Earl Carter becomes president.

1977—Carter pardons most Vietnam draft evaders, numbering some 10,000.

1980—Ronald Reagan is elected president.

1981—President Reagan is shot in the chest in assassination attempt. Sandra Day O'Connor is appointed first woman justice of the Supreme Court.

1983—U.S. troops invade island of Grenada.

1984—Reagan is reelected president. Democratic candidate Walter Mondale's running mate, Geraldine Ferraro, is the first woman selected for vice-president by a major U.S. political party.

1985—Soviet Communist Party secretary Konstantin Chernenko dies; Mikhail Gorbachev succeeds him. U.S. and Soviet officials discuss arms control in Geneva. Reagan and Gorbachev hold summit conference in Geneva. Racial tensions accelerate in South Africa.

1986—Space shuttle *Challenger* explodes shortly after takeoff; crew of seven dies. U.S. bombs bases in Libya. Corazon Aquino defeats Ferdinand Marcos in Philippine presidential election.

1987—Iraqi missile rips the U.S. frigate *Stark* in the Persian Gulf, killing thirty-seven American sailors. Congress holds hearings to investigate sale of U.S. arms to Iran to finance Nicaraguan *contra* movement.

1988—President Reagan and Soviet leader Gorbachev sign INF treaty, eliminating intermediate nuclear forces. Severe drought sweeps the United States. George Bush is elected president.

1989—East Germany opens Berlin Wall, allowing citizens free exit. Communists lose control of governments in Poland, Romania, and Czechoslovakia. Chinese troops massacre over 1,000 prodemocracy student demonstrators in Beijing's Tiananmen Square.

1990—Iraq annexes Kuwait, provoking the threat of war. East and West Germany are reunited. The Cold War between the United States and the Soviet Union comes to a close. Several Soviet republics make moves toward independence.

1991—Backed by a coalition of members of the United Nations, U.S. troops drive Iraqis from Kuwait. Latvia, Lithuania, and Estonia withdraw from the USSR. The Soviet Union dissolves as its republics secede to form a Commonwealth of Independent States.

1992—U.N. forces fail to stop fighting in territories of former Yugoslavia. More than fifty people are killed and more than six hundred buildings burned in rioting in Los Angeles. U.S. unemployment reaches eight-year high. Hurricane Andrew devastates southern Florida and parts of Louisiana. International relief supplies and troops are sent to combat famine and violence in Somalia.

1993—U.S.-led forces use airplanes and missiles to attack military targets in Iraq. William Jefferson Clinton becomes the forty-second U.S. president.

1994—Richard M. Nixon dies in New York City.

Index

About the Author

Zachary Kent grew up in Little Falls, New Jersey, and received an English degree from St. Lawrence University. Following college he worked at a New York City literary agency for two years and then launched his writing career. To support himself while writing, he has worked as a taxi driver, a shipping clerk, and a house painter. Mr. Kent has had a lifelong interest in American history. Studying the U.S. presidents was his childhood hobby. His collection of presidential items includes books, pictures, and games, as well as several autographed letters.